A
Rookie
reader®

Flying Butter

Written by Patricia Trattles

Illustrated by Gary Swift

Children's Press®

A Division of Scholastic Inc.

New York • Toronto • London • Auckland • Sydney

Mexico City • New Delhi • Hong Kong

Danbury, Connecticut

In memory of my parents, Bill and Marge Falsey, who will live forever in the hearts of those who loved them.
—P.T.

Consultant

Eileen Robinson
Reading Specialist

Library of Congress Cataloging-in-Publication Data

Trattles, Patricia, 1954-
  Flying butter / written by Patricia Trattles ; illustrated by Gary Swift.
    p. cm. — (A rookie reader)
  ISBN 0-516-25150-3 (lib. bdg.)   0-516-25280-1 (pbk.)
  1. English language—Compound words—Juvenile literature. I. Swift, Gary. II. Title. III. Series.
  PE1175.T73 2005
  428.1—dc22
                                        2004009162

CHILDREN'S PRESS, and A ROOKIE READER®, and associated logos are trademarks and or registered trademarks of Scholastic Library Publishing. SCHOLASTIC and associated logos are trademarks and or registered trademarks of Scholastic Inc.
1 2 3 4 5 6 7 8 9 10 R 14 13 12 11 10 09 08 07 06 05

Can butter fly?

Butter flies?

Butterflies

Cat fish?

Catfish

Horse shoe?

Horseshoe

Fire flies?

Fireflies

Light house?

Lighthouse

Tooth brushes?

Toothbrushes

Rain coats?

Raincoats

Toe nails?

Toenails

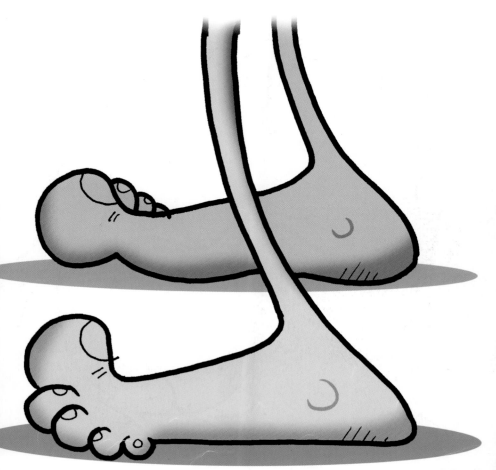

Dragon flies?

Dragonflies

Bookends?

This book ends.

Word List (31 words)

book	ends	nails
bookends	fire	rain
brushes	fireflies	raincoats
butter	fish	shoe
butterflies	flies	this
can	fly	toe
cat	horse	toenails
catfish	horseshoe	tooth
coats	house	toothbrushes
dragon	light	
dragonflies	lighthouse	

About the Author

Patricia Trattles plays with words from her home in Holland, Michigan, where she lives with her husband, David, and their two daughters, Erin and Leah. This is her first book with Children's Press.

About the Illustrator

Gary Swift was born in a small town in northern England. He always wanted to be an illustrator, and has been illustrating professionally since the age of fifteen. He still can't believe that he gets paid to draw funny pictures for a living. He works with clients all over the world with the help of his computer.